Stage Movement

Teacher Edition

By

Tracy Brooke

Stage Movement

Student Objective: Students will demonstrate effective staging and movement during student led performances.

Lesson 1 Stage Composition	Lesson 2 Focus and Staging	Lesson 3 Onstage Movement	Lesson 4 Stage Movement	Lesson 5 Stage Business
Lesson 6 Blocking	Lesson 7 Stage Diagram Review	Lesson 8 Performances	Lesson 8 Performances	Lesson 8 Performances

Employ stage movement consistently to express thoughts, feelings, and actions
Define and give examples of theatrical conventions
Analyze a character from a script: physically, intellectually, emotionally, socially
Develop and practice stage craft skills
Analyze and apply appropriate behavior at various types of live performances

The notes and ideas in this unit are extracted from:
<u>Theatre Art in Action</u>, ed. Lisa Abel, NTC inc, 1999, pg 20, 128, 144-145, 178, 182-183, 231, 252-254, 384.

Stage Movement
Lesson 1: Stage Composition

Objective: Students will demonstrate knowledge of basic stage composition and body positions by performing a three minute improve for the class.

Section 1: Intellectual time

Student goal: Worksheet

Teacher goal: Lecture notes.

Section 2: Game Play

Game 1: Students will perform a cross with different motivations. Teacher will give instruction making sure the students are open to the audience during the crosses.

Game 2: Students will cross to center stage, pantomime and activity and then exit the stage. Other students will guess what the pantomime is.

Game 3: Students will play what are you doing? Two students stand on stage. One student starts pantomiming an activity. The second student asks, "What are you doing?" The first student says something entirely different from the activity they are pantomiming. The second student starts pantomiming the answered activity. Then the first student asks, "What are you doing?" and so on....

Game 4: Each student writes a silly question to an "advice columnist. Partner up the students. One student reads their question. The other person comes up with a name/ title as the advice giver. After the question is read, the second person gives the answer to the problem. Then they change roles, the first becomes the advice giver, the second becomes the advice seeker.

Section 3: Scene Work

Students will have a copy of this work in their student work book.

Scene Work

    Choose a Scene Partner

    Choose a Scene

    Read the script three times

    High light your lines

Section 4: Assessment

Students will create a three minutes improvisation demonstrating good staging and body compositions.

Stage Composition

The Stage Picture

After reading a play for fun, visualize each scene and imagine all the action of the play. Think about where actors and actresses will enter and exit. Imagine their movements on stage. When you put movement into the play, think of it as creating a series of photographs that tell a story.

1. **What are three things you should imagine when you begin to stage a play?**
   Entrances, exits, movements on stage that tell the story.

Stage Positions and Grouping

When you are on stage make sure you do not block other actors from the view of the audience. Make sure that scenery and staging does not block you from the view of the audience. Pay attention to where you are on the stage and do not stay in the same spot for too long. Also, notice your body posture, what you are doing with your hands. Do not play with your costume or hair or space out. When it comes to positions and groups on stage, the actor speaking is the one who has the focus. Do not walk during someone else's lines. Speak, and then walk or walk, and then speak.

2. **What are two things that can block the audience's views from a performer?**
   Other actors, scenery and furniture

Three Basic Performing Guidelines:

1. Cheat Out. This is when you pivot on your feet so that your body and face are toward the audience and still able to see the other performers on the stage.

2. Give A Scene. This is when you cross downstage and turn upstage so that more of your back is to an audience. This naturally takes the focus off of you and the audience will look at the person you are looking at. Giving a scene can also be considered taking yourself out of a scene.

3. Turn the scene in. Actors who are not the key characters in a scene "turn the scene in" when they shift the angle of their body towards the main character. This helps the audience to focus on the main person of the scene.

3. What does it mean to give a scene?

When you turn your body so that the audience sees most of your back. The focus is on someone else.

4. What does it mean to cheat out?

This is when you turn your body so that the audience sees most of your front. The focus is on you or shared with another performer.

Sharing the Stage

One position commonly used for scenes between two actors onstage is called a shared position. Both actors stand on the same plane in a one quarter position. Same Plane (on the stage the same distance from the audience.) One Quarter (feet are pivoted slightly towards the person you are speaking to but most of your body is open to the audience. Shared position – both people are in equal focus of the audience.

5. What are two characteristics of sharing a scene?

Two performers stand on the same plane and in a one quarter position.

Upstaging

When one actor is upstage of another on a proscenium stage it is called upstaging. Upstaging forces the downstage actor to turn away from the audience to communicate with the upstage actor. (Up stage is farther from the audience. Downstage is the stage area closest to the audience)

Once in a high school production of Grease, Two performers were suppose to share the scene DCS. The male performer kept taking a step upstage to force the female to turn her back to the audience and give him the scene. She would then counter and take two steps upstage. He would get mad and take three steps upstage! The two performers were so concerned with being the lead that the play flopped and a great scene became two performers "upstaging" each other. If this were to happen to you, I would suggest a creative solution. What does your character want and what are you willing to do to get it? Then find a creative stage movement to get your goal. Perhaps cross the stage to a prop or something…..

6. What is upstaging? Is this usually good?

When one person moves upstage and forces downstage actors to turn away from the audience. Usually no this is a way performers "steal a scene"

Definitions

Levels: A level refers to the height of an actor's head onstage. The actor who's higher then everyone else has the focus. The actor who is on a lower level then everyone else has the focus. Using different levels creates a creative scene that is more interesting to watch.

Planes: A plane refers to the different depths onstage. The farther downstage you are, the more focus you receive from other characters.

Triangles: When there are three or more people talking, performers should avoid standing in straight lines or just clumped together. Most actors and actresses will attempt to stand in triangles where each point of the triangle has an actor standing on it. This keeps all three people open to the audience and sharing the scene.

Body Posture

Sit, Stand, and move with good posture. Know your posture, learn a neutral posture, and then learn through observation other people's types of body posture. The posture of a character is determined by age, mood, attitude and the relationship between characters.

Stage Movement
Lesson 2: Focus and Stage Composition

Objective: Students will demonstrate knowledge of who has scene focus by creating a set with a strong focus point.

Section 1: Intellectual time

Student goal: Worksheet

Teacher goal: Lecture notes.

Section 2: Game Play

Game 1: Students will play telephone. Three performers sit on the stage behind a telephone. All three talk softly in their conversation. The first performer gets louder and carry's on a conversation, they gradually soften their voice while the second performer takes a word out of the first performers conversation, gets louder and carries on a very different conversation. The third performer takes a word out of the second performer's conversation and gets louder and does a very different conversation.

Game 2: Students will play the restaurant game. Three different tables of performers will pretend to be in a restaurant. The first table will carry on a conversation, the second table will take the focus and the other two tables will turn the scene in.. Similar to the telephone game.

Game 3: Ferris Wheel. Two chairs are places side by side to create a ferris wheel on the stage. Two performers will each take a chair. About twelve kids total. Each have a different description and perform a scene in the ferris wheel. The ferris wheel gets stuck when the scenes begin. Practice taking focus and giving focus.

Section 3: Scene Work

Students will have a copy of this work in their student work book.

    Scene Work

  With your scene partner

  Mark the inciting incident, find the rising action, mark the climax, mark the conclusion

  Break your script into beats of action

  Rehearse each beat of action three times. Each time, experiment with different objectives and motivations.
  Rehears your scene once focusing on the rhythm of the play following the spark of the inciting incident, rising up to the climax and bringing the scene to its natural conclusion.

Section 4: Assessment

Students will create a sketch of the set for their scene. Each group will create their set and go through their scene in front of the class discussing set considerations and focus points.

Focus in Regards to Stage Composition

In terms of stage movement, the focus is the intended point of interest onstage. Directors coach actors in line deliver and movement based in part on the knowledge of how audiences focus and respond to movement on stage. Every stage picture should emphasize the characters that are most important at that moment in the story. Pay attention to the arrangement of people, the dialogue, and the action. Directors strive to get an aesthetic quality to the stage pictures that they create. They want the stage composition and movement to be balanced, evoke certain emotions, and support the story telling of theatre.

   1. What should every stage picture emphasize?
   The performer that is most important in that moment.

   2. What should the stage composition and movement be:
   Balanced, evoke emotions, and support the story

Three Main Types of Focus

Direct emphasis: Focus of the stage picture is on one actor.
Dual emphasis: Two different but equal focuses are on the stage
Diversified emphasis: Frequent change of focuses between five or more people

Body Positions

An actor in a dominant position is the one who is moving or talking. Strong body positions naturally get the attention of the audience members. Full front is a very strong position. This is when your entire body is directed toward the audience. Full back is traditionally a very weak position since none of your face is toward the audience. This can be a very strong position in the right scene and at the right time. If I were directing a scene where military men came to tell a mother her son died in war I would have the mothers back to the audience because I want every audience member to be able to see themselves as that mother. Other story lines could use the full back position to evoke emotion and tell the story in a powerful way. The one quarter position is used most often between two characters who share the audience focus and are equally important in a scene. The three quarter position is used most often in giving the scene to another character. This position is the weakest to stand in because most of your face is directed back stage and not to the audience.

3. **What performer is in a dominant position?**
   a. one who is moving and talking
   b. full front, one quarter

4. **What performer is in the weakest position?**
   The three quarter position where most of your back is to the audience.

Stage Areas

The most natural flow for entrances will be stage left. (that is how we read so entrances and crosses from left to right flow naturally for us) Entrances from Down Stage Right Up to center stage is a very confrontational entrance that will stir the audiences without knowing why. (This is opposite of the flow of our eyes – moving right to left. This is a diagonal line which is forceful and moving right to a person is powerful.

Center Stage is traditionally a very strong position because it is visible to the entire audience.

Down Stage Center is very strong. This is because it is most visible and closest to the audience. Scenes which are emotional and important are usually placed closer to the audience.

Awareness of your positions relative to other actors onstage is just as important as awareness of your position relative to the audience. When you are planning scene movement, be aware of what your position says about your importance in the scene, what it says about your relationship with the other actors, and what the audience will see and feel when viewing the scene.

5. **When you are planning a scene what are two things you should keep in mind?**
   a. What is your relationship with the other characters.
   b. What will the audiences see and feel

6. **How would you have a robber enter to steal an old lady's purse?**

7. **Where would you stage a love scene?**

8. **How would you have the hero enter to save the day?**

Other People and Props

A character framed by a door way, window, arches, or pillars are going to draw more attention than other characters. A character who is on a higher level will draw more focus. A character who is separated from a group of people will have more attention. A character who is farther back stage with other characters closer to the proscenium arch will have more attention.

9. Who will draw more attention a performer at a higher level or lower level?
Higher

10. Who will draw more attention a group or one person away from the group talking?
Person talking

11. Who will have more attention a person framed by an arch way or a person looking at them?
Person in archway

People and Space

Two characters far away from each other suggest hostility or strangers. Two characters standing really close suggest intense or friendliness. Putting a prop or set piece between two characters may suggest some sort of conflict or obstacle in the way of relationships.

Stage Movement
Lesson 3: Common Onstage Movement

Objective: Students will demonstrate knowledge of basic stage composition by creating a series of pictures to tell the story of their scene

Section 1: Intellectual time

Student goal: Worksheet

Teacher goal: Lecture notes.

Section 2: Game Play

Game 1: Freeze. One person sits on a bench. A second student approaches the bench and strikes up a conversation as a crazy person who thinks he or she is someone else. A student might be an alien, a priest, or a ballerina. Students can freeze in at any time, take the place of the crazy person and become anyone…. When you enter the scene know what you want and play this want.

Game 2: Have the students pantomime a list of four or five things to do such as getting ready for bed or for a trip. This time add a reason why they are doing that activity, escaping, punishment, best trip in the world…..

Game 3: "Selling". The class is alien and does not understand English. One student must ask to buy an item like a tire or a radio. They must use body language and sound effects to get the class to understand what it is they need to buy.

Section 3: Scene Work

Students will have a copy of this work in their student work book.

Scene Work

With your scene partner do the following:

Discuss the theme of the play.

Discuss the setting of the play.

Create a set design

Create a series of pictures that show your story line. (see Worksheet)

Practice your scene three times with entrances, exits, and standing in the positions of the pictures you created

** sitting in scenes means that the performer must put out more energy to be as effective as performers who are standing in scenes.

Section 4: Assessment

Students will improvise their scene where each actor moves at least three times.

Common Onstage Movement

Certain movements onstage should be practiced so that audiences believe in the character you are portraying. These movements are entering, exiting, crossing, sitting, and standing.

1. **What are common movements on stage?**
   Enter, exit, crossing, sitting, standing

Entrances introduce your character into a scene. Prepare for the entrance before you come on stage. Before you submerse yourself in your moment before, make sure your costume and make up look right. Make sure you have the right props for the scene. Know what your cue for entering is and make sure you can enter at the right time. When all the actor's tools are ready, then focus on the moment before and submerse yourself into the world of the character.

2. **The dual role of the performer is to think about actor techniques and the character needs. What is something the performer must do to prepare an entrance as the actor and one thing as the character?**
   a. Is costume, makeup, props ready
   b. submerse self in the moment before

If your scene calls for movement with walking up or down steps, sitting or doing something, practice those movements with your lines a lot so that you can execute the movement naturally and effortlessly. You want the movement to be second nature so that you can focus on your wants and getting them met.

3. **Why should you practice your movements?**
   So they look natural and effortless.

Entering in a door way. If you can enter and pause in the door way to deliver your line, this is very effective. If a group is entering have the speaking person enter last so that they do not have to turn away from the audience to deliver their line.

Exits are just as important as entrances. Leave the stage with a definite purpose of where you are going. If you speak when exiting, turn back and deliver the line while still holding the door knob etc…. Find a reason to open up to the audience to deliver the exit line.

Interactive Onstage Movement

1. One character moving towards a person standing still.
2. One character moving away from a person who is standing still.
3. Chase: One movement moving toward a person who is moving away.

Moving toward another character implies that the moving characters wants a confrontation or an emotional connection with the other person. Moving away from the other person says you are avoiding the contact or confrontation.

Always find ways to motivate the movement keeping the plays theme and characters wants in mind. Every movement sends a message to the audience. Keep the movement moving towards the plays goal.

Do's of Stage Movement

Do open a door using the hand nearest the hinges and close it with the other hand.
Do enter the stage with your upstage foot first so that your body is turned downstage
Do cross downstage of furniture or characters who are standing
Do cross upstage of seated characters
Do make gestures with the upstage arm
Do move forward on the upstage food and kneel on the downstage knee
Do sit with your feet and knees together unless you are playing a character who would not.
Do stay in character when leaving the stage. You should stay in character way off into the wings.

Don't of Stage Movement

Don't block an exit while waiting to enter the stage or stand in front of a back stage light that might cast your shadow onstage.
Don't move during important lines, a laugh line, or while the audience is laughing
Don't cover your face with your hands or with a prop
Don't cross your knees or feet or spread your feet apart with the knees together unless your character would do so.
Don't grad the arms of a chair to push yourself up unless your character would do so.

Stage Movement is like creating a series of pictures that tell a story

Draw stage pictures that you and your scene partners can create to tell the story.

Explain the stage pictures created in the space under the picture.

_____   _____

_____   _____

_____   _____

_____   _____

_____   _____

_____   _____

Stage Movement
Lesson 4: Stage Movement

Objective: Students will demonstrate knowledge of basic stage composition by writing their blocking in the script and discussing with teacher.

Section 1: Intellectual time

Student goal: Worksheet

Teacher goal: Lecture notes.

Section 2: Game Play

Game 1: Each of the students will think of an animal and how it moves. A student is chosen to go first. He or she will go to the front and begin circling around the playing area as that animal. When others are certain they know of the animal the student is playing, they will go up and join him or her. When the "herd" is the entire team, the group winds a point.

Game 2: Students will pantomime a walk through. Walking through jello, walking through a desert, walking through a forest, etc…

Game 3: Patterns. The students arrange themselves on the stage floor in any pattern open to the audience. When everyone is up on stage they freeze. Then rearrange into another pattern. Pattern can be at a restaurant, bus stop, dance hall, work location….

Section 3: Scene Work

Students will have a copy of this work in their student work book.

>**Scene Work**
>
>With your scene partner do the following:
>
>Write three to four movements per performer
>
>Choose a prop to use for your characterization
>
>Draw a light bulb where revelations and discoveries are
>
>@ at turning points or changes in action
>
>Practice your script keeping in mind the stage movement guidelines in today's reading.

Section 4: Assessment

Students will show their blocking to the instructor

Basic Movement

An actor is similar to an athlete. Both must have control over their bodies. Adequate rest, proper exercise, regular hours, and good food are needed to keep actors healthy and in good condition – similar to an athlete.

Rules and definitions of movement

Movement should be motivated. Shuffling your feet, scratching your arm and fidgeting movements distract the audience from the purpose of your scene. Motivated movements are powerful, propel the action forward and make the characters dynamic as they fight for their wants and needs.

1. **Why should movement be motivated?**
   Powerful, propels action, supports characters wants

2. **What are unmotivated movements?**
   Shufflings, scratching, figeting…

Movement should be simple so that the audience can see it, understand it and stay with the action of the overall play.

Movement should always be open to the audience. Always "play your scene" to the audience.

Movements should adjust to the other characters on the stage.

It is always more forceful to move toward the audience or toward other characters then away from them.

3. **What are three things movement should be on stage?**
   a. simple
   b. open
   c. adjust to others

Crossing

Crossing is to move from one place to another on the stage. If you are talking and walking the audience will watch you walk and not hear you talk. Stand still during important lines. Move and then talk, or talk and then move. Pay attention to who is moving and talking by thinking and formulating ideas in your mind about what they are saying and doing, just like in real life.

    4. What is crossing?
    Moving on stage

    5. Should you walk and talk at the same time? Why
    Audiences watch movement not the talking. Talk then move or move then talk.

Cross upstage of seated actors and cross downstage of standing actors. Make your cross a slight curved pattern so that you are open to the audience when moving.

Sitting: Make sure you are sitting full front or in a one quarter position. Don't look directly at the chair before you sit down. Feel for it with the back of your leg and then sit. If you look at the chair, so will the audience. Sit comfortably but in a position that you can stand up easily. Sit modesty. Keep your feet and knees together. Standing is more forceful than sitting. Seated characters must expend more energy to build a scene.

Gesturing: Always use your upstage hand so that you do not cut yourself off from the audience. Do not cover your face with a prop or hand movement.

Turning: Always turn toward the direction of your down stage hand so that the audience sees your face.

Entrances and exits: Come on strong and in character with motivation and purpose in a way that is timely, open to the audience, and well rehearsed.

Sets and Furniture: Do not stand to close to walks of furniture. You want to stand out from the set, not blend in.

Upstaging: Unless directed to do so, don't upstage yourself or another actor.

Counter Cross: For each cross onstage, there is usually a movement in the opposite direction by another character. This is called a counter cross. It does not have to cover a distance equal to the first move. Crossing and counter crossing are important parts of rehearsing. They must be carefully worked out so they look natural. Counter cross easily and naturally when balancing a scene with another performer.

Stage Movement
Lesson 5: Stage Business

Objective: Students will demonstrate knowledge of props by using a prop in an improve of their scene

Section 1: Intellectual time

Student goal: Worksheet

Teacher goal: Lecture notes.

Section 2: Game Play

Game 1: Visualize yourself walking into a room. What can you smell? Is the room old or new? You notice a desk in the corner. Is it a small or large desk? Is the wood bright and polished or old and warn? You notice a letter poking out of a drawer. What sort of paper is it? Is it lined or stationary? Is it fresh or has it been there for a while. Take the letter out of the drawer. Open it up and read it. Wait a minute. You fold the letter up and place it back in the drawer. Notice the resistance of the drawer as you close it. You look around the room and walk out. Listen to your foot steps as you walk out of the room. Picture yourself walking up to the school and into this room. Now open your eyes and look around.

Game 2: Each student will be given a person such as a hair dresser, a banker, a grocery worker…. They will pantomime the person and the class will guess who the person is.

Game 3: Entrances: Give a student a place to walk into. They are a doctor who just received the test results going in to explain them to a patient… or a burglar who is entering a house. Have the students pantomime an entrance.

Game 4: Joining in. One student begins a scene pantomiming an activity. When another student figures it out, they come and join in. Continue adding three to four students. Example would be a rock band. One student starts with a guitar and so on…

Section 3: Scene Work

Students will have a copy of this work in their student work book.

    Scene Work

    Check off the boxes when you and your scene partners have completed the work.

- o ☐ Read the scene. Use the "Bounding Ball Improv" You can only speak when holding a ball. Throw the ball to your scene partner during or after your line. This helps the actor learn to connect to their scene partner.

- o ☐ Read the scene and use the "contact" Improvisation. You must make physical contact in an appropriate way with the actor you are speaking to before each new speech, or sentence. This helps the actor learn to connect to their scene partner.

- o ☐ Read the scene and use the "packing pistols" improve. Pretend to fire guns while you speak. This improve helps the actor know who they are speaking to and convey what you want.

- o ☐ Read the scene and then do the "tennis" rehearsal. Swat pretend tennis balls as you speak. This improv helps the actors pick up the pace and achieve a normal pacing for conversations.

On your own

- Write down your objective for every beat of action

- Write down your obstacle for every beat of action

- Write down your tactics for getting what you want for each beat of action

Section 4: Assessment

Students will improve their scene in front of the class with a chosen prop.

Stage Business

Stage business is an essential part of acting and involves the use of hand props, costumes props, stage props, other actors, and even parts of the set (doors, windows, lamps). How you handle a cup and saucer, a pair of glasses or a handkerchief will be different for various characters you portray. It takes a lot of practice to learn how to handle a prop effectively as a given character. Historical props such as swords, fans, and canes need a lot of training to handle properly, naturally and to convey the inner life of the character.

1. **What is stage business?**
   Use of props to portray character and events

2. ___ **T/F Every character a performer portrays handles props the same.**
   F every character is unique and the way they use props reveals their inner life.

Stage business such as writing a letter, drinking from a cup, or poking a stick in a fire takes concentration and practice to look natural and convey the inner life of the character. Good stage business aids a characterization and enhances an entire production. Too much stage business especially out of character or unmotivated is meaningless and distracting.

2. _____ **T/F Stage business should be motivated.**
   T must be motivated and enhance overall production.

3. **What does too must stage business do?**
   Distracts from the character and the play

Eating and drinking onstage present a challenge. Real food is rarely used onstage so an actor needs to imagine with all five senses to convince an audience that the food or drink is real. When you drink hot chocolate on stage, practice drinking real hot chocolate off stage. Write down all the senses and movements and feelings that you have drinking the hot chocolate. Then practice pantomiming the drinking of chocolate milk. Master the skill so that when you are on stage it appears real and believable to the audience.

When you eat onstage:

Do not eat or drink any more than is necessary
Unless the script calls for it, do not deliver lines with food in your mouth
Learn how to dispose of food that is in your mouth – like use a napkin…. In time for your line or movement.

Gesturing on Stage

Imagine a bubble around everyone. This is an imaginary circle that people establish around themselves. Imagine each character portrayed on stage surrounded by a bubble. Each bubble is determined by the personality of the character. Shy withdrawn people have small bubbles. Powerful or daring characters have large bubbles. When you make gestures use the right amount of space within the "bubble" to convey character.

The size of the imaginary bubble that surrounds us is cultural as well as individual. Americans tend to define their space as follows:
Six feet or more is formal.
Three to five feet is friendly
Less than two feet is intimate.

Without being aware of it, people guard their bubble space. Observe people in elevators and busses and how they respond with body language to their bubble space touching someone else's bubble space.

As you work on your performing skills and characterizations, develop a master gesture for each character. A master gesture is a distinctive action that serves as a clue to a character's personality. The master gesture might be a walk, a laugh, or a movement with a hand or prop.

Center of Gravity

Almost every character onstage begins movement or leads with a part of the body that is appropriate for the characters personality. A lead looks as a string is attached to a part of the body pulling that part away from the others. If a character leads with their head they may be a thinking type of person. If a character leads with their chest they may be confident or loving. A prideful character may lead with their chin. Food centered people may lead with their belly. This is considered the center of gravity for the character.

Stage Movement
Lesson 6: Blocking

Objective: Students will demonstrate knowledge of blocking by giving pointers to another groups blocking.

Section 1: Intellectual time

Student goal: Worksheet

Teacher goal: Lecture notes.

Section 2: Game Play

Game 1: Simple Action. Give a student a simple action like washing the dishes or brushing their teeth. They perform the action and the class tries to guess what it is.

Game 2: Two students cross the room and meet in the middle. One person is a banker, the other person is a lottery winner. Another group one can be an old lady and another person is a thug. Give a definite situation for the greeting in the middle of the room.

Section 3: Scene Work

Students will have a copy of this work in their student work book.

> **Scene Work**
> With your scene partner do the following things and check them off when complete:
> - **Step 1:** read the scene and then improve it in gibberish. This helps develop the meaning and messages of the scene.
>
> - **Step 2:** Read the scene and then improv it while dancing. This helps to find the movement of the character based on wants and needs in the scene.
>
> - **Step 3:** Read the scene and then improve it while laughing, crying, or chuckling through it. This improve supports the actor in finding different emotional levels of the scene.
>
> - **Step 4:** read the scene and improve it is slow motion. This improvisation helps you find the moments of pause and deliberateness of the scene.
>
> **On your own**
> - Create a character sketch
> - Create a moment before you enter the scene
> - Create your moment after you exit the scene

Section 4: Assessment

Students will perform their scenes in front of another group and receive blocking ideas and pointers.

Blocking

Blocking is to coordinate all the actors' movements on the stage. You write down your blocking so that you do not forget it. The following symbols help you to write fast and efficiently. Most of the time the actor or actress will record blocking when they are on stage with the director telling them where to walk. Use a pencil so you can change blocking as needed. An assistant director may write all the blocking down in a master script as well.

1. **What is blocking?**
   To coordinate all actors movements on the stage.

2. **Who writes down the blocking?**
   Actors in their scripts.

Use symbols so that you can record fast and keep up with the director.

ent = enter
X = cross
ex = exit
© = The first letter of a persons name is used
bz = business
pu = pick up
st = step
bf = before
... = pause
w/ = with
fr = from

Make symbols for window, chairs, tables and other things that make sense to you and are easy to remember.

If you need to write upstage use a U
If you cross downstage use a D
If you cross center stage write a C
Use an L or R for left or right stage

Remember, it is your script and your blocking notes. Use whatever symbols or picture are easiest for you.

When blocking a scene think about the following questions:

What is your characters personality?

What are your character's objectives?

What obstacles are there?

What are the motivations for your character?

What are the relationships between the different characters?

What necessary action needs to take place?

Where are the main focal points on this set that can be used to high light dramatic moments?

Stage Geography
Lesson 7: Stage Diagram

Student Objective: Students will practice effective placement of objects and people on the stage by pulling out a scenario from a box and then setting up a stage or positioning people on the stage in an appropriate way.

Section 1: Intellectual

Student Goal: Worksheet

Teacher Goal: Lecture Notes

Section 2: Game Play

Step 1: Every one stands in a circle. One person goes into the hall for a second. Choose a leader. They are going to start a movement and everyone else is going to follow. After a moment or two they will change the movement and everyone will follow along. The person is called in from the hall. When they get to the center of the circle, the leader begins the movement. The person in the center tries to figure out who is starting the movements.

Step 2: Improvisation: One student is interviewing for a job to buy something important to them. The interviewer needs to have a clear job that he is looking to hire someone for. Create a stage set up that is appropriate and find two movements for each character.

Section 3: Scene Work

Rehearse your scene and polish for performances

Section 4: Assessment
Students will pull a scenario out of a box and place people and set pieces in the best way for the scene.

Materials: scenarios

Stage Diagram Review

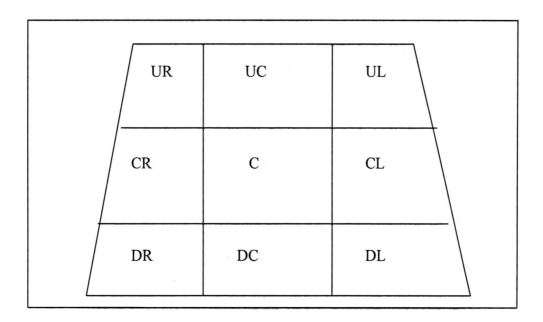

Johann Wolfgang Von Goethe. In 1796 the Duke Karl August asked Goethe to come to Weimar Germany and work as the director of a company. (In this time period you did what the Duke told you to do. Germany was a lot like the different states with no strong federal government.) No body wanted to work in Weimar because it was a bad acting troupe with stupid, uneducated actors and actresses. At first Goethe would not do a thing to improve the acting troupe. After a while, he decided he would turn the acting troupe into something great. So, he divided the stage floor into nine sections to help the actors know where to move on the stage floor. Goethe is considered one of the first directors in the modern sense. In 1817 he lost the director job to the Dukes Mistress.

Remember that the stage areas are created for the actors. It is in their perspective. Right stage is for the actor facing the audience. Left stage is for the actor facing the audience. Upstage is away from the audience. Downstage is closer to the audience.

Dominant Stage Areas

Area strengths for a proscenium stage
CS – strong center of focus
UL or UR is weak. More difficult for the audience to see the action.
DS – strongest – closer to the audience.

Square psychology for set design and blocking
UR square of strength
DL square of finality
DC square of questioning

Area psychology for Set designs and blocking
Good guys enter from RS
Bad guys enter from LS
Audience eyes travel like a book from SR to SL

Body Strengths
Body positions that are strong are ones that are most open to the audience.
People in focus are ones at higher levels, away from groups, framed by the setting i.e. door way, window….

Use as much of the stage floor as you can
Planes – different depths of the stage floor. (US is a different plane than CS)
Diagonals – two actors on a different plan
Triangles – basic people composition of three or more people

Stage geography Review

Draw a stage floor

Who is Goethe? What did he do?

If you want the audience to not know who is going to win the fight, what stage floor position would you put them on?

Back Stage

Square of Strength	→ → Flow of audience eye	→ → →
URS	UCS	ULS
CRS	CS	CS
DRS	Square of Question DCS	Square of Finality DLS

Audience = House, Out Front

Back Stage

Planes – – – – – – – – – Up Right Stage	– – – – – – – – – – – – Up Center Stage	– – – – – – – – – – Up Left Stage
Planes – – – – – – – – – Center Right Stage	– – – – – – – – – – – – Center Stage	– – – – – – – – – – Center Stage
Planes – – – – – – – – – Down Right Stage	– – – – – – – – – – – – Down Center Stage	– – – – – – – – – – Down Left Stage

Audience = House, Out Front

Stage Movement
Lesson 8: Performance

Step 1: Quiz

Step 2: Performances

Step 3: Evaluations

Performance Evaluation

Name: Date:

Category	Points Possible	Points Received	Comments
Set	20		
3 movements per person	20		
Prop and gestures	20		
Good Technique	20		
Memorization	10		
Stay in Character	10		

Performance Evaluation

Name: Date:

Category	Points Possible	Points Received	Comments
Set	20		
3 movements per person	20		
Prop and gestures	20		
Good Technique	20		
Memorization	10		
Stay in Character	10		

Stage Movement Quiz

Name: Date:

1. What are three things you should imagine when you begin to stage a play?

2. What are two things that can block the audience's views from a performer?

3. What does it mean to give a scene?

4. What does it mean to cheat out?

5. What should every stage picture emphasize?

6. What should the stage composition and movement be:

7. When you are planning a scene what are two things you should keep in mind?

8. What are common movements on stage?

9. The dual role of the performer is to think about actor techniques and the character needs. What is something the performer must do to prepare an entrance as the actor and one thing as the character?

10. What is crossing?

11. Should you walk and talk at the same time? Why

12. What is blocking?

13. What is stage business?

14. ___ T/F Every character a performer portrays handles props the same.

15_____ T/F Stage business should be motivated.

14. What does too must stage business do?

Stage Movement Quiz
Answer Key

1. What are three things you should imagine when you begin to stage a play?
Entrances, exits, movements on stage that tell the story.

2. What are two things that can block the audience's views from a performer?
Other actors, scenery and furniture

3. What does it mean to give a scene?
When you turn your body so that the audience sees most of your back. The focus is on someone else.

4. What does it mean to cheat out?
This is when you turn your body so that the audience sees most of your front. The focus is on you or shared with another performer.

5. What should every stage picture emphasize?
The performer that is most important in that moment.

6. What should the stage composition and movement be:
Balanced, evoke emotions, and support the story

15. When you are planning a scene what are two things you should keep in mind?
What is your relationship with the other characters.
What will the audiences see and feel

16. What are common movements on stage?
Enter, exit, crossing, sitting, standing

17. The dual role of the performer is to think about actor techniques and the character needs. What is something the performer must do to prepare an entrance as the actor and one thing as the character?
a. Is costume, makeup, props ready
b. submerse self in the moment before

18. What is crossing?
Moving on stage

**19. Should you walk and talk at the same time? Why

Audiences watch movement not the talking. Talk then move or move then talk.

20. What is blocking?
To coordinate all actors movements on the stage.

21. What is stage business?
Use of props to portray character and events

14. ___ T/F Every character a performer portrays handles props the same.
F every character is unique and the way they use props reveals their inner life.

15____ T/F Stage business should be motivated.
T must be motivated and enhance overall production.

22. What does too must stage business do?
Distracts from the character and the play

Performance Evaluation

Set:
1. Does your set follow the guidelines for use of space, open to audience, focal point.
2. Does your set tell us where you are.
3. Does your performance show us how you feel about this place and the people there.

Movements
1. Are your movements motivated>
2. Does your movements show a series of "stage pictures" moving your story forward
3. Do you fidgit or blank out, are you actively listening and moving naturally
4. Do you stay open to the audience and follow the guidelines taught in this lesson.

Props and gestures
1. Do you gesture with the upstage hand and in character
2. Do you use a prop to show the inner life of your character
3. Do you find something unique to make your performance memorable

Technique
1. Are you open to the audience
2. Do you move naturally and effectively
3. Do you move into focus and give the scene appropriately

Movement Scenario's for Improvisations

Simple Movements:

One student seated CS. Another student enters, first exits, second then sits CS
The friend tells you to go home immediately because of an emergency

Your mother asks you to go to the store to pick something up for the dinner

Your father tells you to take out the garbage.

Your parent tells you to get off the phone.

You tell your parent you wrecked the car

Convince your parent to give you the car

You are told to go clean out the garage

Create three movements:

You enter a shoe store, sit to be waited on.
Describe to the clerk the type of shoe you want. Clerk brings three pairs to you.

You enter the kitchen secretly. Move a chair to reach a cake and get yourself a piece.
A family member enters in a different way, tells you the cake was for a bake sell

You are painting a table when the phone rings. You go to answer it and get in a conversation.
A family member enters and puts something on your table.

You enter an expensive hotel lobby and walk around.
You sit down and notice a person who notices you

You are a a library reading a funny book.
The librarian crosses to you and asks you to be quiet

You are waiting for a job interview. The employer greets you in the lobby and askes you to come into his office

Character Sketch

Physical
This is the first level of characterization concerned with gathering facts.

- Name
- Age
- Weight
- Eye color
- Hair
- Skin

Write memories or events or perceptions and thoughts that you have about these facts.

Your background influences what you do, how you think about things, how you express emotions. Your present behavior is determined by events of the past. Know your given circumstances.

- What do you say about yourself
- What does the stage directions say about you
- What do others say about you

Social
This is the second level of characterization placing the character you created in their environment and in relationship to others.

- Do you have friends, what do you do with them, how do you feel about them
- What kind of family do you come from
- How do you feel about your family
- What was your child hood like
- How do you feel with other people
- How do you feel when you are alone
- What was your education like. How do you view school.
- What do you do for work or an income. How do you feel about it.

Psychological Traits
This is the third level of characterization justifying what you do in the world of this play.

- What do you think about life
- What do you thing about people
- How do you treat people
- Are you an optimistic or pessimistic person, why?
- Consider the way you the character things, fast or slow, simple or complex, creatively or analytically.
- What is your center of gravity?

Moral Behavior
This is the last level of characterization concerning the values and love of your life.

- What is your view on life, what is the super objective of your character
- What is your religious preference
- What happens when people die
- What is the greatest thing someone can do for another
- What is the most horrible thing you can imagine
- What is the most beautiful thing you ever saw
- What are your political view
- What superstitions do you have

Participation Points

Student	Day 1	Day 2	Day 3	Day 4	Day 5	Day 6	Day 7

**Library Days
Student Assessment:**

Student Name:_____ Date: _____

Parent/librarian/teacher supporter: _____

___1. Read a play.

___2. Found a scene/monologue and photo copied it.

___ 3. Got Thespian records up to date working towards honor medal at graduation.

___ 4. Got scene and character sketch scanned and saved working towards portfolio.

___ 5. Got resume and head shot up to date working towards high school portfolio.

Game Day

This is a nice way to find or cultivate talent for the School Comedy Club.

Play students favorite Games

Pattern a class period after the comedy club

Use a resource such as Comedy Sports International and use their game playing agendas.

Anita Jesse's The Playing is The Thing is a great resource for student games.

Theatre Art Relationships

Student Conferences

Scene Work
During the class period it is good to work with each of the groups doing scene work. Asking questions like, "how well do you think you are performing or utilizing the skill taught today? What areas are you struggling in? How did your scene turn out? Did it go as planned? Watching a beat of action and side coaching it is a great way to make sure each student understands the concepts being taught.

Thank You's
Thank you notes to students after performances is a great way to reinforce the positive qualities and growth the individual is making. When I was in high school, we would all eagerly wait for our note from our director and devour them.

Questionable Material
If a student chooses a monologue that does not meet school expectations or is questionable material I will ask to meet with the student after class.

Questionable Behavior
Dr. Ross Green (livesinthebalance.org) has amazing information to support the teacher and the learning environment. His website has a tun of free information and resources. The main thing I learned from him is that teachers tend to focus on the class as a whole, however, when we focus on the individual the class as a whole does better! We as theatre teachers have a unique ability to influence individuals for the better and create life long relationships with parents and students.

Student Tracking

Date: Class:

Check indicates repeated student behavior

Student Name:

	Week	Week	Week	Week
1. Failure to follow instructions 2. Not doing Work 3. No Materials				
Overt Behavior: 1 Defiance/insubordination 2. Refusal to obey 3. Talking Back				
Subtle Behavior: 1. Non-verbal (body Language) 2. Gestures 3. Defiance				
Away from assigned position in room without permission.				
Disrespect student/ teacher / aid				
Secondary Behavior: 1. Posturing 2. Inciting 3. Contributing to others behavior				
Assault / Physical Behavior				
School Rules (clothes, electronics, food)				
Refusal To Take Responsibility				

Teacher Responses:
Verbal Warning:

Student / Teacher Conference:

Teacher Discipline:

Parent / Teacher Conference:

Theatre Arts Behavior Report

Student   Date

      Educational research has consistently shown that when a teacher spends excessive class time managing discipline problems, less teaching and student learning occur. In theatre classes, time is given to individual work which allows the teacher to work one on one with each group and every student. However, the personal training time is dependent upon the entire class being on task.

I regret to inform you that your son or daughter exhibited the following misbehavior during class which prevented a positive education environment:

Failure to follow instructions
Failure to bring appropriate materials
Excessive talk, noise, and/or sounds
Foul or disturbing language
Failure to be in the appropriate place with the correct partner.
Talking and/or not paying attention while the teacher is lecturing
Discourteous conduct towards other students
Refusal to participate
Misconduct during performances
Not taking responsibility for actions or behavior
Unit work not competed nor turned in.

Additional comments and explanations:

_____

_____

_____

Please sign this form and have your son or daughter bring this back to class.
Please call for a parent / teacher conference.

Parent signature   Date

Thank you.

Student Teacher Conference.

1. What behavior is happening that leads to this conference?

2. What do you need?

3. What behavior does the teacher need to maintain a great classroom?

4. What does the teacher need (need underlying behavior)

5. What are three things I can do to help you get what you need (#2)

6. What are three things you can do to help me get what I need (#4)

7. Lets both choose one that we can both do and talk again in two weeks.

Parent Teacher Conferences

Our goal is to be a team with the parents and keep the parent informed.

Informal Meetings
Parents and I would speak at performances or other production meetings or get togethers. Parents would informally ask how their child is doing and usually wanted to know about emotional/social/mental issues. At these informal comments, I usually focused on the positive and gave a supportive and hopeful comment to the parent. I never felt a student was in crisis during these conversations, if I did, I would have asked the parent to come in for a conference.

Thank You's
Parents are the life line for the theatre arts teacher. Make sure you are asking parents to support the program and giving thank you notes for all the help and support given.

Conferences
Keep the conferences during school hours and in a public location.
Have documentation to support the student strengths and areas of concern
Be positive and optimistic – you are talking with people who have devoted an enormous amount into the life and well being of another person.

Before a conference:
Email the guardian the time, place, and purpose. Ask them to bring any question or concern.

During the conference:
Greet the parent at the door.
Give a positive comment about the student and show great work!
Discuss the area of concern
1. Here is what I am doing to support your student:
2. Here is what you can do to support your student:
3. Our goal is _____
4. Lets get together in _____ weeks and see if we are reaching this goal.

After the conference:
Thank you email
Follow up conference

Grade Updates
I am very serious about grading in a theatre art environment. Since most of the class receives a B or lower – I feel it is best to send out grades to parents every three weeks so that no parent is surprised at the grade their son or daughter get. Parents have thanked me. When a flunking grade is sent home, the parent calls other teachers and can stop something frustrating from happening at the three week mark.

Parent Requested Conference:

1. What item of concern do you have for your child?

2.. What item of concern do you have with this production/ class/ program?

   What do you need?

   What does your child need?

   What do I, the teacher, need?

3. What can we do that meets all our needs?

4. Here is a strength, positive contribution your child makes to this program.

5. Here is the grade of your student.

6. Here is where I would like to see your student focus for greater success:

Teacher Requested Conference

1. Objective of meeting:

2. Student Strength and documentation:

3. Student area to grow in and documentation:

4. Any question or concern from parent:

5. Follow up meeting scheduled to see if objective has been achieved.

Before the conference make sure that you....
Make positive assumptions about the student and family.
Know what your goal is and what needs to be communicated
Have prepared materials and documentation ready
Have solution ideas ready.

During the conference make sure that you....
Ask questions to learn about the student
Listen actively
Tell the truthfully

Parent questions:
Is my child doing good?
Does my son or daughter need help?
Can you tell me about how you teach?

Concerns in Theatre:
not doing assignments
not following school procedures
inappropriate behavior in scenes or performances

Tracy Lybbert:

I love writing lesson plans and bringing life and vitality to the classroom experience.

Please write a review and let other teachers know how these lesson plans support your work, your students, and your program.

Please contact me at www.teachingtheatre.weebly.com
I want to hear from you!

What works, what doesn't work?
Like Michael Shurtleff says, Every day we must learn, learn to do good theatre.

Theatre Pictures by Cindy Murray Lybbert
Author Portrait by TAG Photography

Cover Pictures by:
Cindy Murray Lybbert

CPSIA information can be obtained
at www.ICGtesting.com
Printed in the USA
LVOW09s2229150118
563037LV00017B/392/P